Reality Bytes

By Brad James

REALITY BYTES

Meizius Publishing, 2015

www.meiziuspublishing.com

Contents

Rumination 1

Are we prisoners of expression?
Or do we bear it in the manner that Hermes bore tidings to the Gods?
An idea is as ephemeral and enticing as the smoke spiralling skyward from a hookah.

The mission is to find the one.
The one that makes you feel like a Superhero just because he knows your name. He in whom you can see the eternal struggle, the poet's muse, the knight's battle to win the maiden's heart.
Who holds the peace of a thousand ascetics in his smile.

This “one” need not be human at all, merely whatever plays your heart like a harp!

32 and Counting

"Have you seen some cunt that looks like Catwoman on Ketamine? No? Me neither, but it's on my Bucket List!"

This is a thesis, a Doctorate of dossing from one whose hand has been forced by matters beyond him. A life where the sole ambition was to walk forward, in no particular direction, and make the best of it. However, where it's been a solid choice for 15 years, every path - any path - has been sawn off into a sheer cliff. When faced with nothing but oblivion beneath, do you stay on your crag of rock forever, hoping to remain satisfied with the paltry lot that oligarchs have thrown you? Or do you leap, hoping in vain that you land somewhere at least a shred more satisfactory than the edge you are stuck on now?

An eternal gamble of the proletariat. Faced with hardships the posh like to laugh about behind their glasses of fizz, and people on whom they expunge endless energy and pleasure in crushing like the pips in strawberries, floating and pickling in said glass. The fruit has been permitted to wallow in some semblance of opulence and success for a time; the osmosis of the heady, effervescent liquid seeps in and threatens the integrity and structure, weakening it. The insidious grape juice implies to the strawberry that it has gained access to the same level of privilege it sees all around it: "Congratulations! You too, are Bourgeois!"

Of course, the once delicate and beautiful strawberry's integrity has been compromised. Its heady trip in the midst of decadence is now savagely sundered, tipped on its head, rushed as a beleaguered boat that slips dangerously away over the event horizon of a waterfall. Only, these jagged rocks are teeth that dismantle the once delightful fruit, the deeps of the lake/river are the human gullet, where only a pool of acid resides.

Sounds like a ramble? It's not; it's the ideal symbolic comparison to the once promising sweet young flesh of the British working class. We are crushed now, like the strawberry; only our saccharine, artificial fragrance remains, permeating the air and used to perfume our desecrated souls with the illusion of social mobility. 2013 has certainly become an unlucky number! Although we have the power to change what we see fit in a world we all share, watch this space!

We are all Apps in the eyes of the Universe...

"All art is subjective" is one Hell of a contentious sound byte!

City Nights

Dark cities consumed by the light,
The miasma of dark spewed by vice,
Street and head lamps priapic in bore,
Summer night rain dampens, threatens and laments.

Skyscrapers, mountains of mammon, above,
Concrete, rigor mortis rivers, below,
Permeated by people, vibrant souls, but lo,
All exuberance, snatched, by a city's edifice!

Creative Cemetery

Push open the gate to the Creative Cemetery,
Stiffened almost rigid with rusted dreams and petrified ambitions,
Traverse the path cracked by false hope,
Beneath cold night, towards moribund talent, lain out to rot!

A grass verge rears high, to plummet you to earth,
To scale it again, returning fleeting optimism to help you cope,
Though the unkempt greenery, reminding you all is overgrown,
In a place where forgotten people languish in their cold home.

Jagged tombs and stones puncture the green,
Broken smashed memoirs of talent unseen,
Etched into the rock are their tales, deeds and squandered gifts,
Having absorbed the strengths and memory of brilliance.

Past the tombs stands a church to glorify what has gone,
Decayed splendour to mourn and grieve for all that is lost,

An altar for artistry and all squandered for its cost,
To commune with the divine deities of kudos, validation and aplomb.

Perhaps in this hub some shred, mere speck and iota remains?
Take some for myself, pass to others, steal back banality's ill gotten gains?
Radiate the world in beauty, mind's progeny to edify at great pains?
Emancipate creativity, passion and ardour from mundane, heavy chains?

Indifference is insidious, lurking in every place my eye looks,
The biblical serpent slithering, it's hiss stifling thought,
Searching out new victims beyond the banality's boneyard,
To pull those corpses back to its den, bloating the burgeoning necropolis.

Yet it's everywhere I go, the orgy of the carefree careless,
Never looking beyond the nose, or a 16:9 screen,
Unable, unaware incapable of venting their spleen,
At being prisoners, captives of modernity's bromidic regime…

Cyber-Addict

Today, I had an Epiphany,
The Proverbial alarm has started to ring,
It's in my head, clamouring against the cell of my skull
Each thud saying: "how did this happen?"
"How did you get here?"
"Look at what you've fucking done to yourself!"
I've become a willing slave bewitched by the Siren's Song,
Of a wolf in Sheep's Clothing... !
I... am a Cyber-Addict!

I, AI

A world with intelligence and knowledge for all,
A life with a sentience abundant, why run when you can crawl?
I am I, AI, plastic genius and synthetic know-it-all,
The artificial Autarch, silicon Sorcerer, you're under my thrall!

The Plastic Pied Piper, leading you by the nose,
An elixir of life too late, taunting your death throes,
Fleeting, intermittent and tantalising, comes and goes,
Turning minds to mindless, enslavement, it shows.

Out of the depths I cry to you oh Lord,
Save me from the pervasive, invasive, cyber horde,
Sever the dependence, rend me from the motherboard, cut the cord,
Put my mind at rest, peace comes at the edge of a sword.

Veins become circuits, the blood turns to data,
With an influence surpassing the rough hand of pater,
Overriding the nurturing guidance of mater,
Wiping the brain, leaving it fresh with no trace of the traitor!

I've gorged avariciously on abundance, an anti-ascetic,
Bound to this chair, screen, self-afflicted quadriplegic,
Pained, lonely, yet forums and Facebook proves the analgesic,
Well versed and unschooled in cut and thrust dialectic.

Who am I? Me or it? Singular or whole?
Do I matter? Do I mind being trapped in a crowded black hole?
A constituent of the total still means I've sold my soul,
To be mindless, a drone in a colony where no one knows their role.

Welcome to my web based, insubstantial Multiverse,
I am all here, learned and layman, chaste and perverse,
Transcend with me, to omnipotence, experience power in reverse,
Indulge The Hooded Hore, immerse yourself in my verse!

Insert Title Here

Here is some, poetry or even, prose,
Letters, words... something I suppose,
If you have owt better, please propose,
While I languish here in morbid repose...

Vagueness plagues me like a fatal disease,
Despondency drowns me, a slick of sleaze,
Relief only arrives with the force of a breeze,
Only to leave me again, without an if you please.

KIS

Verse can be a curse, yet ignorance is worse,

Go on, spark imagination's match,

Run on, brandish inspiration's baton,

Become one, with knowledge's nurturing bosom.

Labyrinth

A rabbit in a maze,
A junkie in a haze,
Caught in the headlights,
Of my blinding, grinding malaise.

Talking to, walking to, never escaping a brick wall,
Helplessly masochistically wallowing under its thrall,
Looming over me, impregnable, an impenetrable pall,
Leaving me drowning in vile, seeping, creeping gall.

Give me the days when I was once free,
Unhindered to you, unfettered to me,
Too blinded by euphoria to look ahead and see,
Life has other designs, fashioned by Harpies.

Where is the way out? The exit? Pot of Gold?
Have I right to bargain before my life is sold?
Knowing my fate before I even grow old?
Unwelcome, uninvited, uninitiated into a hostile fold?

This winding unending trap is my birthright,

The progeny of a class that has had to fight,
For scraps of rights, unendingly with no end in sight,
Lacking champions to take up arms to aid our plight.

Why not sit back and except my fate?
Make the most of my lot before it's too late?
Because I need my life in flux, not in one state,
I wish to chalk up variety to my thus far bland slate!

Freed from this prison dictated by birth, heritage and class,
To navigate mountains of possibility by a narrow, tenuous pass,
In reality to reach no higher than the blades of grass,
Because in Britain, all and sundry are ruled by class!

So here I remain bound in the labyrinth, trapped,
Stifled, stumbling my energy sapped,
A well that has run dry of potential untapped,
Rotting on a cold stone floor, all I am broken, snapped.

Level 9

How, please tell me do we be free?
Why do you say we must be ugly?
What have you done to our chemistry?
Where did you stash the vibrancy?

Drag me down to Level 9,
Convince me that my soul is not mine.

There are my eyes to help see,
The darkness enveloping me,
My choices are now paltry,
No true and clear destiny.

Drag me down to Level 9,
Convince me that my soul is not mine.

Life

Life is fought and won from day one,
A battle fought from the mother's gauntlet run,
To waltz with heartache and a dalliance with fun,
An osmosis absorbing everything under the sun.

Like You?

Hey you sitting over there,
I like the style of your hair,
Turned on by what you wear,
I could be like you if I dare!

The Macrocosm of Me

Where I live, is a reflection of me, my core, my being,
Southend, of what? The bottom, of the barrel? South facing in the sun,
Exposed, vulnerable, tough and ugly, rough and ready,
Full of fun and overrun, from living too fast and being burned by the sun.

Nestled on the cusp of the sea, beyond the reach of the city,
Limbo town, halfway between here and there, coming or going,
Privy to more twists, turns and drama than the tides,
Witness to ebbs and flows, sex, drugs and rock n' roll.

Buzzing with the scraps of humanity, littering pavements like...
Soggy chips, waiting to be picked off by eager seagulls,
Where opportunistic pigeons and birds seek scraps and
Shrapnel, for just enough sustenance, just enough booze.

Take a gamble down the front, then barter with your life in tenements,

Thrill yourself on a roller coaster, or dive, or cheap strip club ride,
All part of one organism, a varied, gaudy and heady package,
Seared and scarred under glittering lights and dilapidated grandeur.

I see my reflection everywhere round here,
In Boho bars, museums, rotten kebabs and stale vomit,
Alone on the isolated end of the pier, more bumps and scrapes than dodgems,
In more slips than the seaweed and more shifts than the sand.

Everyday I start anew, re-open, a Kursaal with each sunrise, only to,
Close down, like a busted old Marina, Victoria Ave's old offices,
inhabited by a sole cleaner, that's all there is, I wish I could be keener,
But a dead-end town does not a live man make.

I'm a Barometer, swinging between old pier planks to new developments,
They tell of the war within me, and the earnest will to be me, and be free,

Try to fit, to be comfortable, with myself, in all my horrific
guts and glory,
A little like Southend, the resort, town and cautionary story.

Mask

Tragic visage smeared behind a mask of fun,
Decaying skin, dead attractions rotting in the sun,
Legions of losers, lemmings leaping, one by one,
Towards release, where their lives come undone.

Each one deteriorates with the fabric of time,
Unravels and frays with no reason or rhyme,
Awaiting for something which is vague and sublime,
Desiring answers to life, one odd puzzling paradigm.

An overspill, ghetto that's been raped of all pride,
Descend each level of Hell on our Helter Skelter slide,
Witness dignity recede, swifter than the eager tide,
And feel sense, decency and taste desist, it doesn't abide.

A pier juts out to sea to avoid ill fame,
Detached, deserted, destitute, out of the game,
Derisive, disdainful of the splendour turned lame,
Resigned to the fact that it will remain forever the same.

A coastal melting pot, rendering fat of social slurry,

People, to and fro, frittering away lives without a worry,
Mired in sinking currents in ignorance, no need for hurry,
Skulls scour their minds, with more activity in rush and scurry.

This is home, we call it Southend-on-Sea,
Where degradation, desperation and despair roam free,
Where reason, dignity and civilisation flee,
Where wishes drown in bile and brine, no soul hears their plea.

The Masses Are Masochistic

The masses are masochistic, thick, narcissistic,
Begging for the Jack boot of the Bourgeois on their nuts,
Pleading for waterboarding beneath a barrage of the banal,
Turned on by the torture of misplaced culpability.

Miasma

Miasma, so sickening, creeping and infusing my plasma,
inside, a virus, outside, a lengthening shadow,
a ghost, spectral remnant of a bolder self,
the Poltergeist of previous zeitgeist, lapsed in time.

This noisy spirit screams in my mind,
a bull in a china shop with my nerves,
stampeding the shattered fragments of strength,
Lame oxen, in vain, tugging mud-trapped wayn,

The bull is crippled with fear,
anxiety rendering heart, tissue and sinew powerless,
While the wayn of hope offers whispers a way out,
Is mired, aimless, sinking in marsh of mental malaise.

The mud reeks, the blood seeks,
a way, any way, to pump out the poison,
Mind's a masochist, life the sadist,
existential manacle, chaining pain to the falling rain.

Modern Mirror

Here I lie in the palm of one "users" hand,
Inanimate, encased in synthetic sentience,
Wires imbue my being as imitation veins,
To the nerve centre, the chip, heart/crystallised sand.

Mirror, Mirror

Mirror mirror in my hand, where in life do I stand?

Mod

Saviour's sedition, the featured edition,
Of his/her, our condition, our whinge, our rendition,
A world void of ambition, full of suspicion and partition,
An intravenous junkie, hooked on omission.

Modern Foxhole

Always crouching, never slouching,
I don't have time for that, they could come anytime,
Vigilance is the eternal price of freedom,
In a warzone, in a Modern Foxhole…

… Sentry duty, the watch never ends,
Patrol rounds again, respite from restlessness,
From the worry of knowing they're round the corner,
Preying on your prayers for salvation.

Here I stand, individual, sole, technically "free,"
What freedom is achieved with no release?
From bonds of financial strains that seldom cease?
Grinding you down, raping you of peace!

Exit from the foxhole seems perpetually barred…
By wire, mines… useless paraphernalia,
Mostly by the sticky red tape of bureaucratic procedure,
Furring destiny's arteries with dense deprivation.

They win war with attritional degradation,

Draining you like the leeches they are,
Allowing them, the warm-bloodied, soft-hearted lump you are,
Until you are left a cold relic of your "viable," "employable" self.

National Poetry Day

Today is National Poetry Day, so I'll give rhyming a go,
Wax lyrical, ditch reason, go with artistic flow,
Be creative and thoughtful and get on with the show,
But still languish in mediocrity, not permitted to grow.

Arts floundering, apathy flourishing,
The masses stifled, starving, never nourishing,
Beneath the heel of the bourgeoise languishing,
Huddled, tarred under one banner brandishing.

Where does Britain go from here what's it's path?
Shall we let the rich destroy it just for a laugh?
Subject it's beauty to Oligarch's wrath?
Rob you of all but the least to survive, to spare you half?

Notes

Writing is mental screaming at the screen,
audible as the attainment of art,
etched on the cave, scrawled on the page,
Wings of the eagle, manumission of the slave, soul
remembered on the grave.

Nouvelle Vague

We are the Nouvelle Vague, far from fey,
On the pulse of a vibrant life, this is our time,
Blind to the behind, ignorant to forward, so they say,
Yet their MO I praise, for the purposes of this rhyme.

The Opiate Soul

Gather round, but beware the lure of The Opiate Soul,
A being with currents deeper than any can know,
Screaming roaring from a deep none fathom,
An echo reverberating through an empty addicted shell.

Imbibe deeply from the heady bong of love,
Permit ephemeral mystery snake to the core,
The comedown is wondering what you're here for,
A rhetorical rumination, rendering you bruised and sore.

Rehabilitate with a life lived, loves loved, ventures gained,
Act as if your existence is rebellion until society is drained,
Endeavour is the watchword for society to be stained,
Disavow oppression, or you will be pained.

Pigeon 1

It comes to something when you envy a pigeon,
Those reviled, rancid, avian rodents,
The bats of beggary, feathered diseased destitute,
Shunned to buggery, sifting through shit.

Yet a pigeon has wings, a pigeon can fly,
Spurned ignored, unfettered and free,
At liberty to exploit our avaricious profligacy,
Supping on our slovenly superciliousness.

An opportunist, an optimist, getting by on the sly,
Infiltrating society, pilfering through poverty with aplomb,
Saluting society with a middle finger and irreverence,
Fracturing the norm with the need to just be.

Pigeons

We are all of us pigeons, down to a man,
Treading the tiles in the plumage of our profligacy,
Ignoring the ingrained dust of destitution,
Young males strut, puffed up chests and necks bloated with ire,
Pursue indifferent females who don't turn a feather,
Only to hatch more slaves and scavengers to the 1%,
We flock to this mausoleum metropolis, museum to mammon,
Clipped wings by the Fuhrer fancier of capitalism,
Punishing all for our collective doom…

… One and all, slaves to the daily grind,
Disallowed for trying to use our mind,
Though our base is vast, revolution in every disinterested gaze you find,
Fly pigeon, run! Flee, take wing and never look behind.

Pleasure Beach

Pleasure Beach, where our primal selves meet the sea,
Dancing on a threshold, mingled minds and moulds,
The land calls you home, but ID balks away,
Answering the rhythm of high tide, sailing your soul.

Poem

I teeter on the knife edge of crystallised dreams,
Chiselled shrapnel, fragments from a broken soul,
Frantically searching for the remnants of my life,
Desperate to piece together rhyme and reason for being.

The Sea

The sea, oh dark, frigid, cruel sea,
Darkest depths, salty, turbulent, unrelenting sea,
Coring, washing, bleaching, revealing the deepest of me,
Siren tide, tugging yearning, enslaving and setting me free.

Enveloping, seeping and sapping liquid, leeching life,
Purging away the excuse of my life, washing clean strife,
Cutting away ego, baring the vein of truth, like a knife,
Yin to land's yang, husband to its wife.

Sentient Circuits

Imagine if you were not truly free and never had been. Choice and individualism, all dependent on your place and time within the universe, like cells in the body. This is the basic workings of the universe. All intelligent life are constituents of a meta-intelligence, which is the Universe itself, as is every universe in the multiverse complex. All of which are hyper-intellects competing for the something further.

Serf

I am a commodity, floated and flipped for a profit,
where is my eternal serf's cap, I need to doff it!

Shopping Cart

Descartes in a shopping cart,
virtual slavedriver, you're whipped down to an art.

Sign on for Your Supper

Sign on for you supper,
Beseech the rich for more,
Their derision makes you scupper,
Feeling more debased than a whore.

I am a Job Point for all sorts of slung mud,
Universal Job Match for decimated dignity,
Your sanctioned psyche is politician's cud,
Fit for fictitious work, beneath freedom or pity.

Sour Sixteen (From Falling Hope)

A girl can think she is a Queen,
When you are a young teen,
The world hasn't yet lost it's sheen,
When you're sweet, not sour, sixteen.

Storms

Storms we cannot weather,
Life we cannot tether,
Flightless as a feather,
Death's heady scent of heather.

All a ruse, forcing one to comply or die,
Pastiche freedom that the soul knows to be a lie,
A scream of protest too hoarse for a sigh,
Objection to liberty, starved, abused and left to die.

The mind is free, disallow any shackle,
Reality is a circus, a clown's callous cackle,
Juggle your mind and soul, their conflicting crackle,
Mortality awaits, feel it in your hackle!

Surcease the Clowns of Love

Surcease the Clowns of Love
and clip the wings of its maimed dove,
set a soul free, force doubt to flee,
unite the shattered pieces of you, and me.

Jesters of romance dance upon graves,
Matters of heart manipulated by knaves,
Harlequins toy and fool with sinner and sin,
jingling bells of misery, a patchwork din.

Time

Time is inexorable,
Somewhat exceptional,
Always expendable,
Never consensual.

A soul is flexible,
An entity endurable,
Elation and ennui merely temporal,
Insubstantial as it remains indomitable.

I Try Too Hard

It was one of those days, grey cloud smothered the sky,
Throwing a jealous veil over the sun, covetous cradle,
One time I thought I knew which way I was heading,
Along a turnpike, writhing with the serpents of self-doubt.

Self-doubt is an elixir freezing your vital thoughts,
A callous demon that forces you to try too hard,
When you have talent in spades piled in your backyard,
And you choose pretension and/or ignorance as your trump card!

You know a writer like you is a dime a dozen,
What makes your nuance and verbal dance so strong?
Is there something in your own air instilling gifts, secrets,
Perhaps your tortured soul knows? Plucking your harp strings?

Are you a minstrel in an abandoned court?
The kings all overthrown, any queen taken,
wrenched by mediocrity's mummer's farce,
Seized by banality's raiders, insidious invaders!

There was a time when you could have it your way,
Way back when, empty words, echoing refrain,
They resounded too much and are residual, inane,
The covetous cradle, nihilist, plays the winning hand again!

The sun set on that day, a fleeting flirtation with skill,
Light snatched from my bubble to flounder in failure,
A bosom cold, unyielding, giving no quarter to you,
Welcome to redundant night, blacker than your apathy!

Veil

A veil is made to cover and obscure,
Beneath it I hide, scurry, and try to forget,
The sickening evil rotting and scouring me, once pure,
Corrupting the soul, leaving a shell, residues of regret.

I fled there, a pilgrim seeking salvation,
Imploring God, beseeching him, them for peace,
The answer to my prayer is further degradation,
For me, it's pain, not wonder, that will never cease.

What Is A Page?

A page is a crucible, forging weapons of words,
The razor sharp wit of poetry and prose,
Thrusts and parry capping steel halberds,
Bloodshed of ink parodies the heady scent of a rose.

A page is a battlefield, valiant and craven,
Shells and shrapnel form verbs and vowels,
While a reader pores over sentences like a raven,
Hunting meaning, seeking eyes within cowls.

A page is a ballroom, filled with ladies and lords,
Waltzing with reason and rhyme, beat of the room,
Ensnaring reader with every shriek of the chords,
Eternally unfolding with ardour of bride and groom.

A page is a cosmos, abundant like Earth, barren like Mars,
Tale akin to motes of dust, or myriad minds of men,
Stories to chill like a void, or illuminate you like stars,
Books more varied than where or when, now and then.

Winter World

The snow glazes over all and never melts,
A chill deeper than you know,
The frost is in my veins now,
And it will stay, rot and grow.

Ice can crack but freeze over once more,
Chill penetrates deeper than any knife,
Raping you of freedom, clarity and energy,
Rendering your soul frigid with fear, paralysed by despair.

Do you even recall the summer sun?
The freedom of a deep blue sky?
A day of liberty that made every fibre soar?
Clear, wide expanse where opportunity filled all routes?

Festering fetters of thraldom have forced your hand,
Urged rigor mortis to claim you where you stand,

Snowed in beneath the subsumption of your class,
Ennui of entropy and bare branches all the same,
Workfare for the workshy ploughing away the drifts,

Salting your grit with propaganda and shit!

Everyone longs for spring to come,
Ice thaws for others, never for some,
Awaiting warmth, heart's hitch-hikers' thumb,
Winter's won, you're froze there, struck dumb!

Shelter by the Sea

Don't tell me of darkness, because you don't know,
Don't mention pain, shame, dread, hunger or hate,
Don't think of me, pity me as you stomp me down,
Don't see or hear me, touch me, taste my bitter pill,
Because you don't know me and you never will.

I sit, alone, out of the rain…for now,
A shelter by the sea, one home of many,
Is my canopy, sanctuary, roof over my head,
The view is priceless, and I am worthless,
A vista teeming with life, and watched by the dead.

Feed me, I hunger nourishment none will give,
Bathe me, absolve my past and sins, purge memory away,
Clothe me, dress my wounds in bandages, adorn me in your empty promises,
Save me, rescue me from the Hell of my life,
Forget me; leave me to wallow and sink, immersed in my strife.

Give me a day with some daily bread,

A day without cold, damp, sickness or dread,
Swap my cardboard box with a bed instead,
Find me a way to deal with the shit in my head!

Lonely, free, purgatory on a majestic balcony,
You laugh, you stare, you don't fucking care!

Nobody!
Farm Animal!
Bedlam-by-the-Sea!

To you...I may be dead, ever in your sight, always out of your head,
I ask for change, you demand ignorance!
Then again, don't feel sorry for me...I have my Shelter by the Sea.

You Deplete Me

To my dearest Carly. How did it come to
this? I never imagined I would end up
losing you! All the time we spent together,
we had good times and terrible times!

You and me against the world, how we
triumphed, defeated the odds through
thick and thin, you alone became my
kith and kin. From our first dance under
disco lights, I clutched you like no other.
Dizzy heights, shocking lows, shining stars,
dirty gutter.

It was only you that could lead me astray,
dragging me to back alleys, as comfortable
there as a black tie soiree, dancing as you
did there, the moon our cabaret…

…You made me strong, stronger than steel,
no one could break me under your spell.
Then you could pull the wool and the rug

away, trashing me, dashing me, I was a
third wheel! Only you saw through to the
truest of me, at my best, at worst,
as a prisoner, but still roaming free…

…No one else believed in you, only me,
NEVER THEM! It was never you that did
any wrong, only me, NEVER YOU! They
told me to walk away, told me you were
bad news, they are the bad news!
They're the ones that give me the blues! I left
you and now you're leaving me! Why…?
Why…? Never can anyone else understand
what we have! Why…? Why…?
WILL YOU NOT COMPLY?! All we've
done together! Say you will
try…don't leave me cold,
cosy up in bed with me at night,
say you will try?

…Our battle scars, but who wins?
All I know…is you deplete me…!

As of Yet Untitled

I am going to spirit myself away,
To avoid my horror, despair and pride,
Let me be the ghost lost in the fray,
Forgotten until some distant turn of a tide.

Valour is teasing, spiteful and cruel,
It turns a blind eye at one's greatest need,
Rendering you bereft and broken and ran out fuel,
For insidious fear to fester, grow and breed.

Chariots of Ire

Here they come, the Chariots of Ire,
As racing and speeding bullets of rage,
As an ephemeral, inflammable consuming pyre,
They last merely a heartbeat, yet linger for an age.

It's scar tissue extends even to your bones,
Seeping and creeping into your very soul,
Saturating the psyche, to multiply, expand, make clones,
Trapping you in a void, in a formless black hole.

Is there an end, where is the source?
Can one seek peace when chaos rules?
Wrench control from an unknown force?
To become an island amid an ocean of fools?

Genererous/Disingenuous Vanity

Vanity, sweet vanity, twinned with insanity,
Capricious building block, pernicious wrecking ball,
Master of illusion, ingenuous cloak for clarity,
Lifting you higher than them all... though pride comes before a fall.

Believe me, being vain is a real pain,
Hurting, griping, judging and sniping,
Regarding others, and yourself, with disdain,
Hidden behind slap and false idols, never eradicating the sting!

All this concern with how you look,
Concerned with the praise, praying for no blunder,
Why not try reading a fucking book,
Because nothing matters when you're 6 foot under!

Wake up, stand up, wise up to what really matters,
The body is a temple, but the mind is the altar,
Be meaningful, be something, before beauty shatters,
As it surely will, with age, the looks will falter.

Enter the Open Spaces

Enter the open spaces, what do you see?

Is there a way back to you? Or a way back to me?

Green Dot

Little green Facebook dot,
what have you got?
A friend? Foe? Memory to cherish?
Or to be forgot?

It pops up unbidden of its own volition,
dealing out either dread or joy, lacking contrition,
a reminder, constant barometer of the human condition,
ardent in dereliction, anti-anthropocentric mission.

The status, the poke, the like, the comment,
this is your God now.

Intelligentsia

We are the intelligentsia, we are so smart,
We contemplate, ruminate, cogitate, our recurring part,
Constantly debating and meditating the wisdom of Descartes,
Meanwhile, ransacked beds masquerade as high art!

We nurture a nature none but ourselves intended,
Engineer a structure, unwavering, complex portended,
Fashion faux culture from stray lace, beauty distended,
Forget fleeting existence, a philistine therein, extended.

As You Make It

We are the makers of dreams,
Movers and shakers of timorous themes,
This is a bastion that will not fall away,
A fad that will last you more than a day.

What else? What more, is there to say?
That dreams and hopes last more than a day?
I wish, yearn to quell fears that none can allay.
But that would be one more lie that entered the fray!

Poem 2

Hard up, fed up and set up, which way is up?
All I can see is down, mired in mud, with malaise in my blood!
Caught in the inertia of my own indifferent daze,
Will I? Will the world, move on from this insouciant phase?

When I write these lines, stanzas, words and verses,
Do they have merit? Do they have meaning? Are they merely mental cleaning?
What gives the rhyme and motion more cogency than curses?
What permits money, status and looks more meaning?

How exactly did the world ever err?
When did our spectacular fall from Grace occur?
Meaning, matter, life grows to an indistinct blur.
As culture, beauty, nature and life starts to slur.

I feel my poetry is beginning to sound the same,
Then again, am I really to blame?
Due to my schooling, class, caste, I've been elbowed out of the game,

Desperate for escape, doomed to this trap, forced to be tame.

Am I prisoner of something else?
Intangible, unimaginable and overall inconceivable.
Under the thrall, beneath a Hex most deem unbelievable?
The need to feed, a drive of gluttony, sating said is
unachievable.

Welcome to the Colony

Ignorance isn't Bliss !
Ignorance is dangerous !
Knowledge is Power !
Knowledge is our Saviour !

Welcome one and all to the Colony,
Ants we are, uniform are we !
Marching inexorably towards the common goal,
Where is our soul? How are we free?

What Does It Mean?

What does it mean, truly mean, to be Human?
Is change as constant as it is ephemeral?
Is life, love and evolution eternal?
Will there ever be peace that is truly fraternal?

Who am I? Is the question of questions?
Where am I? Is the wonder of wonders.
What am I? Is the mystery of mysteries.
Why? Is the blunder of blunders!

Histories and mysteries stretching back unbound,
Is time manmade? Or fabricated, stitched in, covering, every dimension?
Am I free? Or a prisoner without direction, hope or intention?
Are we merely lickspittle sentience, a test, an invention?

What To Do?

Where oh where did it go so fucking wrong?
Wondering when my life went for a song?
Why, I said why must I drag myself along?
What to do, to break through the smog of the throng?

A while ago I dreamed a stupid, fruitless dream,
Dreamed I could be whatever I see or seem,
Yet dreams are intangible, weightless, wisps of steam,
Reality tears through them, a scarring, marring, destructive beam.

My ambition's hemmed in by a Police Blockade,
Determination is slowly beginning to fade,
I've been had, fucked over, unscrupulously played,
And no one will ever come running to my aid!

This, boys and girls, is the state of the nation,
Length and breadth, no hope, no future, that's our vocation,
No one will listen, no one will care, or heed our proclamation,
Yet we are one, we are legion... and a Lost Generation!

Outrospective

Don't you envy the prisoner? Does not some shred of pity abound in a frigid soul? Despite contempt proving the overwhelming assessment of their life on a skin deep cursory evaluation? However earnest in the race to extricate any iota of similarity, you deliberately overlooked the shared affinity with the inmate. Failed to realise your own intangible incarceration over their apparent one?

Reality Bytes with the venom of snake! Bytes as vampiric teeth into a cookie, dental memory banks registering taste for the whole, synthetic enamel, offering up flavour to the motherboard altar.

Reality Bytes

Reality Bytes and illusion stings,
Both writhing snake pits of innumerable things,
Where imagination or desolation sprout wings,
Staying motionless as an aching heart sings.

Massacre the minutiae of your life for the Minimum Wage,
Allow the agents of corruption to attach an arbitrary gauge,
Disavow freedom, love, truth, curiosity, peace and rage,
Wallow in the wilderness of the worthless, lobotomised sage!

Sitting here solidly, the sole owner of your sentience, free?
Alone against the world, tangible you and never we,
Blind to all but a screen, why can't you see?
The Universe beyond your profile, of which you always be?

The air you breath, joy you feel, pain you ignore, doesn't cease,
Or push the boundaries of your inner peace,
Or hire out your freedom on a strict lease,
They merely sustain your existence, a recalcitrant crease.

What to do with this time and space?
Entering rapids, how to master the race,
Confront the things you are unable to face,
Enrol in real life, our true saving grace.

Ergonomic Posturing

Insurmountable difficulty of sitting well, perennial slouching,
A perpetual problem of the chained masses, tidally locked,
partially blocked from the osmosis of natural symbiosis,
forever cocked, Russian Roulette attention from cyber
"friends."

Text Poetry 1

I am Piggy, hear me squeal!
Force feed me nothing but rhetoric swill,
feasted on by bankers who wish me only ill,
My offal tossed away, yet they crave more still!

Text Poetry 2

The entire nation is back in recession,
perhaps that's the reason for my utter depression?
Or did I somewhere get the wrong impression?
All in all it's a matter of digression...

Text Poetry 3

Have a great night!

Take my sunlight,

Shine and be bright,

and give my soul flight.

Text Poetry 4

Welcome to Britain, degradation nation!
Where hopelessness and despair are stops at your station,
Where few can afford even the price of indignation!

The Ghost

Sometimes I lose focus of things, lose sight of my purpose,

At other times I wonder if I should be here at all,

Then there are times where I believe.

I Have a Meme for That!

I have a meme for that, they call it emulation,
They call it culture, or viral inflation,
It could be deemed foolish, vapid stagnation,
It serves the purpose for millions' gratification.

It conveys the zeitgeist in a neat little package,
Smoke signal for emulation, heedless of damage,
You laugh at the joke while munching a sammige,
And pass on to your peers with the conviction to renege.

Take Us to the Vets

A soldier is entropy personified,
Ordered vessel meting out chaos,
Armies deal in maximum collapse,
Laying waste to land, corroding culture,
The MOD's model...

... Now you, the disseminator of disorder is done,
Ready to be flung, in the wasteland,
A dump where the veterans flounder,
The dead receive adulation as heroes,
Even nothing is deemed too much for us...

50 Shades of Fey

A marsh, mire, lethargic pyre ravishing meaning,

Vagueness claims all.

Universal Credulity

Coming from a town a hair's breadth from Hell,
battered jacket, tatty Giro, string frayed at both ends,
where he was running to or from he couldn't tell,
a study in poverty, default shame, most awful of trends.

What is a job's worth? Far more than I'm worth!

When you're a reject, expelled from both ends of life,
vagrant of vagrants, faunal flea from the scrapheap,
poverty cuts and blunts more than the edge of a knife,
talks, words, the world and life is naught but cheap.

Death mocks birth, I see the sky though I'm far beneath the earth.

I am an escaped prisoner of the ism causing a schism,
at odds, opposed to supposed Darwin's condition,
freedom's the dwindling light from an inverted prism,
downward spiral, slinking, limping into perdition.

Roiling in inequity's surf, moored in failure's berth!

What am I worth? What are we worth?

Shame on Whom?

No matter how fast you run,
Shame always runs faster,
No matter how you venture into the sun,
Shame's shadow extends farther!

Cultural Construct

Back when the world meant something,
I had wings gifting me flight,
Back when money meant nothing,
Freedom to think and question was a God given right!

Listening to Chopin while internet shopping, business trouncing beauty,
Leading a charge of two opposing models, turning your head as they career head on,

Don't educate, eviscerate,
Forget to ameliorate,
Only remember to excoriate,
Trade love in this free market, for hate.

Insurrection Is Not a Default Installed Option

Facebook etiquette is a tenuous thing.

Apocalypse is a Trending Topic

Society's so anodyne, I need an Anadin!
A revolutionary's more infidel than Saladin,
Falling before a lance borne by zeitgeist's paladin,
Though in your cage, see the stars, lay back and grin.

Celebrity banality, messiahs of social nihilism,
Centre of conceited Monoverse, study in solipsism,
Is there owt worse than your conceited vampirism,
Sucking the lifeblood of nurturing collectivism.

Pop culture has an axe grind, a tie to bind,
A wish it won't grant and eyes to blind,
Paths to lead you down, a way back you won't find,
Forever searching for more, a worker's prison for the mind.

Saccharine Circuitboards

Electrical impulses all sticky as syrup,
Flooding the neural pathways, synthetic sugar rush,
Sweetening sour lack of interaction,
Cloying cyber circuits of liquorice for you to munch on mindlessly.

If We Deign to Care

If we deign to care,
If we dare to go spare,
Should we dance mon frère?
Jig fast and loose with all that's fair?

Fair or foul, governments growl,
A fight when humanity throws in the towel,
Unity is eviscerated straight through the bowel,
You're too sedated to scream out and howl.

Archiwreckture, Housing the Modern Lecture

(Written in the shadow of a modern breezeblock of
educational enterprise)

Here I sit, education's ennui,
Before a slab of caustic causality,
Arc to culture and arts, forgotten within,
Minutiae of vast knowledge, minuscule under,
Altermodern altars, praising the 'business' of learning.

To quantify the quanta of learning,
To tame the beast of curiosity,
To tame the wild tempest of discovery,
Is something a cage of Archiwreckture will never do!

Despite the overpowering stench of smug satisfaction,
The bins outside still overflow with the discarded pupae,
Of human vermin's vittles', proving the apes anarchy to earth,
Reminder that endless metaphysical shelves of wisdom,
Always fall afoul of base waste!

Creation as Motion

Creation as motion, musing as art,
Philosophy birthed by dastardly Descartes,
Taught to challenge boundaries,
Tautology scorning flare, ability.

Though I deign pretension and whim,
I still long for the presence of him,
A yearning of potent 'gay' vigour and vim,
My sundering from love is what makes me grim.

Swelter by the Sea

There is no shelter to or from the sea,
No competent buffer barring the ID from me,
No hiding place from fervent society,
That has tamed mindless want seamlessly.

Libroleum

Do the structures we build,
Dedicated to the pursuit of knowledge,
Possess an unspoken requisite,
Suffusing their steel and stone?

Are these obligatory assigned spaces,
And architectural vacuums to emulate,
The vacuous?
In our ever expanding (slowly) knowledge?

iPhone Home

There is something artistically tragic,
In walking past a desolate shop,
Replete in it's abandon by sporting a
"iPhone for sale here" in the window.

It's in this ghostly window,
We see our burgeoning spectral selves,
A pastiche of the freedom we so avariciously squandered,
In heady pursuit of cyber coke, the Smartphone,
Opiate of the Window's generation!

Quantum Eugenics

People want it all, but all is a lot,
Split a tiny atom and what have you got?
Quantum off tap, quantum on switch,
Countless iota of reality all digging a ditch!

People like drivel, it rhymes with dribble,
Salivating slime softening all in it's path,
Tenderising tendrils of tautology taught,
Before it digests celeb sewage in egress.

A faceless sea of papped androids,
Energy boost to their banal circuitry,
Cyborgs of synthetic fervour and fear,
A binary we wish to play second fiddle for.

Friends on Benefits

They gather in a royal procession,
Less than ants, servile in destitution,
Begging for scraps of gruel from a punishing regime,
No ears to hear you disembodied scream.

Amputated Android

Searching for the severed, atrophied attachment,
Trying to short the circuit of spent solitude,
A man cannot be an island in the 21st century,
But instead lost amid oceans of profile and data.

To be cruelly sundered from the cyber scene,
Parodies the pariah, neither special or specious,
Cramped in a world where interaction is spacious,
Being without, atrocious, within, gracious.

Autumn Ups and Leaves

Autumn's petrified leaves fall to earth,
Society emulates by stripping me bare,
Measuring, assessing some arbitrary worth,
Casting me aside, one of myriad spares.

Mall Flanders

A bench is a trench for a marooned soul,
Overwhelmed in the heady surge and capitalist charge,
A bastion to ponder: "where did I go?"
Amid saccharine neon glory, proclaiming the demise of liberty.

Watch the Naked Ape gesticulate,
Perambulate and shriek,
At the wares in a moribund jungle,
Where nature rehashed painfully to form friezes of conformity.

A place where even light has been stymied from natural speed,
Socio-economic slurry roiling in a mocha latte cup,
Whipped up froth, pastiche to the,
Pond life drinking it.

Soul Canteen

A soul in a tin can, thrown in a hole,
Mechanised abyss, AKA being on the Dole,
Lower in zeitgeist's estimation than a miner shovelling coal,
JSA leech, lowest of the low, akin to paedo, or internet troll!

These muddy waters of morality in which you swim,
Imbibing desolate fulfilment to your brim,
Stuck on a roulette wheel, spun to statesman's whim,
Convinced you deserve a life even more grim.

Trees shed leaves in autumn, you shed dignity all year,
Rotten fruit of superiors saturate you as they jeer,
In stocks of class, don't you dare shed a tear,
Weep inside, bind yourself in shackles of fear.

A dole scrounger, is there a tale of more woe?
Than being Britannia's pox ridden ho,
To flounder in the wide spaces in which you're free to go,
But liberty is a luxury not for you, you know?

Cross Rails

A station is a nation amid changing borders,
Of people press, business mush,
Disputed territories of home and trade,
A nation on the move, a populace staid.

Electric veins of mass transit abound,
Mobile sardine tins of human goodness in flux,
Charging ahead with purpose unmapped,
Unrivalled, unfettered, uncaring, unrelenting.

Connecting to areas otherwise sundered,
To climes different in a divided nation.

Death Knells and Rock Sticks

We sell death knells by the sea shore,
Washed up, fucked up… thanks tides nevermore,
Nature supplicates before 'progress,' who's the whore?
Humanity's the stake, ruined, whether win, lose or draw.

Pink sky above pale page, here, I am all,
Superfluous nothingness, frivolous idleness,
A page makes use of my visions', rendered silent now,
Assimilating minutiae of myriad monotones.

A human is an engine with nowhere to go,
Aching a drive, spin, speeding gung-ho,
Motionless light speed, sonic vroom,
Return to source, minus inertia or course.

Brains glow in the dark with a plethora of ideas/ideals,
Lighthouse signalling for a kindred to rush home,
Fraught beneath rocks yearning to snag and tear,
At a soul, a look, a thought, a hair.

Work Fare Well

Farewell to alms, healing's gone now,
Snatched to dab sweat from his lordship's brow,
Dashed to pieces like a doomed bow,
Misguided by the Siren of enterprise... Machiavellian Sow!

Farewell to alms, it's final curtain call,
Pulled around, a bed stuffed with cash and all,
Prepared for the head of the rich man... temporal,
Reminder of a past when you were healed, the gall!

Food (Wank) Bank

I open my mouth to speak and my eyes to see,
Eyes absorb the light, ears suck in sound,
Yet for the mouth to take in nourishment has become criminal,
Worthiness to eat, a trial the poorest are set, albeit subliminal.

Words can educate, life can edify,
They bestow energy in their own, unique way,
It fails to replicate food in energy imbued,
A power a freedom, insurrection the elite misconstrued.

A food bank tries to stave away starvation,
But perpetual frustration lingers in the eyes,
of those bound by callous limitation,
Unable to stem a swelling flood is their defeated implication.

Futility suffuses the old church hall,
Dank odour of adulation turned rancid, like my last parcel,
All that's left is a pack of dried noodles cloying to a shelf,
A study in regressive evolution all to itself.

An ology in degradation, poverty and punishment,

Thesis on the failed Capitalist construct and vicarious blame,
Heaved by hungry, their souls craving more than food,
Whipped by elite, telling them freedom does more harm than good.

Impoverished vessel staggers past a glittering store,
Convenience not the order of the day for one who is poor,
Aisles of fair fare, rendered foul by pecuniary censure,
Eternal excoriation, drip feeding the jobless dementia.

You deign to steal from this metropolis of meals,
and are snatched yourself, to answer for your audacity,
To beg absolution for wanting more, to dare to wish for repleteness,
Your pleas bypass compassion, another dent in one's incompleteness.

You now belong to the food bank crowd,
A gathering of those too destitute to be proud,
Whose lives are masked by an acidic shroud,
Scouring away dignity until your sense of freedom is cowed!

Remonstrance

Washed clean by the burning sun,
A life's work over, yet never begun,
Casting eyes frantically for a place to pray,
Knees buckling beneath the weight of day.

Scream to empty lungs and fill one's soul,
Hope's flight lower than broken wings of a gull,
Plummeting over frozen attempted clones of me,
Drowned at sea, in acid lies of the punchline: "I am free."

Dazzle of the blackness obscures a way out,
Paralysing restlessness of tortuous doubt,
Caricatured existence reverberating there & here,
Lame with the crippling shockwaves of fear.

Remonstrance of our simplicity, pillaged, burned,
Ashes craft a labyrinth where those lost cannot be turned,
Lungs ache from screaming out echoes insane,
None can heed wails of the guinea pig's tortured refrain.

Geoff

Only in death will I be truly free,
No expectations, zero holds no weight,
A foundation to the vacuum,
Plunging depths deeper than a wrist's slash.

Life is barrier, a cage, a court and you the felon,
A body like a capsule awaiting existence's acid digestion,
No sedative for the wicked as void's acid dissolves,
Making you whole again, drowning in the fervor of morbid fever.

Of

Of ideas that splash and cascade wantonly on yielding fabric of potential,
Of moments, sparks and ice shards, punctuating the green of the mundane,
Of life's oil slick, it's rough sand texture, that parody carousel,
Of feeling, exceeding static, far short of tempest, lurking to dye cotton of normalcy,

Of heartbeats, organic clock chimes rapping out Morse Code of wonder,
Of motion, perpetual, temporal cadence, a swathe incisive across paper matter,
Of senses, an orchestra performing the symphony of mind's curiosity,
Of love, the ultimate journey, the means to all ends.

Dichotomy

Nectar of ideas drip, genesis of action,
Pooling as blood on reactionary paper of doing,
Tangents divide, forks in the lightning of thinking.

With fervent passion I bud like cherry blossom,
Waltzing to the caprice of sun and breeze,
Yet I calcify, harden and crack beneath winter's savage
discipline.

Rendered motionless alongside frost choked tundra,
Too petrified to wait for scents of blooms,
Splashes of rain, or a breath to claim as my own.

Life’s Rush

Life is fought and won from day one,
A battle fought from the mother's gauntlet run,
To waltz with heartache and a dalliance with fun,
An osmosis absorbing everything under the sun.

A Letter to a Prisoner

Calligraphy on dead trees, a letter to an enveloped soul,
Floundering, bewildered narcissus, blooming alone in the bare Necropolis,
Amphetamine roots snake through and revive moribund soil,
Lulling cloying damp caged air and bound soul with illusion.

Ink, still wet, paints a masterpiece, gushing sanguine light through bars,
Penstroke Panopticon of postponed possibility, warden to your life left off,
Yet words and the page themselves are a cage, impeding liberty to imagination,
Solitary recollection, hard time for the spirit, nonchalant outside sees & raises pain.

A letter to a prisoner is a tunnel bored from a vacuum,
A redundant remonstrance and muffled howl of one incarcerated in society,
Where in unison we are all pages rent and severed from the mater tree,

Leaves unturned, pages unfallen, littering invisible paths to manumission.

Communiqué from one stir to another,
Hard labour as jail time remains at another's pleasure,
Walk the Mile of modernity, a Bedlam that melds commoners and pariahs,
And none are ever free.

Bewonderment

Sickness glistens in the teardrops of protean mourning,
Aching for halcyon gold of the meadow's sway,
The embrace of capricious sunlight that spills and fractures,
On the cornfields of ordered society and motes of unwhispered secrets on ears.

Yet that would make you me, a vinegar slick on fractured wounds,
A cloudy nebula of bewonderment, infusing moonbeams and woe,
A duel gloom of offered sacrifices to joy and meaning,
In a world where no such leap of faith is lost on anyone.

There are spiders in my nightmare for you, in the dank places,
An empty space where I "like my own status" yet dare to tread further,
Bewonderment chases me with glitter as teeth, abandon as tongue,
There are no lies in the blanket of your soul, or ties in the tears of the whole.

Fragmentation

Shards of indecision fragment my soul's wake,
Choices imbue sand and flotsam upon my shore,
What of the savage boons we grant ourselves?
Beseech their vengeful finality, insert profane hope.

Past under a microscope of unrelenting scrutiny,
Hindsight's glare, most spiteful of man's curses,
What if? A thorn deforming beauty of every day's rose,
Might have been, cracked veneer in forward motion.

Halcyon haze descends, fogging truth and sentiment,
Misting banks ghost, poltergeist from yesterday's sea,
What jetsam breaks upon tomorrow's spectral herald?
The future is tenuous, rocky is a path none dares to tread.

Shells of ourselves are discarded along the reality of the shore,
We, faunal crustaceans, implore for more sheltered meaning,
What now? Resounds the cavernous recess of fresh sanctuary,

Awaiting portended bombardment, winds and tides of the next.

Gasp

Gasp empty lungs at the setting sun,
Scream deaf hopes and shadows at the sky,
Placed under a capricious thumb,
Soul's wilderness refuses to quit, lest it die.

I have no shoes or bruise to wear away,
Little to choose over silent refrain,
Shoot a gun from the excuses I pray,
Mugged into thinking there ever was aim.

Breathlessness the thrall of fate's hoar frost,
Panting as a drunk against the unfeeling bar,
Intoxicating soul sell never imparts the cost,
Yet rolls out a path for the con of near yet far.

The brothers-in-arms of thick and thin,
A warrior class, their code stricken and bare,
Hardy, stoic in the face of their own dread sin,
A dead-end awaits endeavor mon-frere.

Take up arms on the head of a pin, see what bursts,

Lacerate a difference of dust and lace,

Beg for the rain, for the feel, the thirsts,

Fate is denied, choice withheld, on dread's grace.

Gasp lungs at the bejewelled, coy eclipse,

Glare blind dreams and rapture at the night,

Release pressure on the force that slips,

And hurls edict at existence, marring fight and flight.

Kill a Man's Giro

Bureaucracy's mountain, pierces levels like a sore lesion over poverty's savannah,

Intense heat of oppression beats tribal pulses dragging you forward, unwilling,

Locusts and grasshoppers hiss censure in stalks of swaying grass tenements,

A feral scope of nature's aggression, seized, compressed by boundaries of red tape.

Predators circle fringes of the stage, eager teeth ripping flesh of morale,

Hyenas toy with your carcass of hopes and dreams,

Persistent drought envelopes, days blend into relentless struggle,

Nights see you holed in an unyielding hovel.

Transpose what transpires from plane to bedsit, you, gazelle,

Hid amid minutia of nothingness awaiting devouring by lioness' of civil service,

Mountainous glory is banished into edifice of government office,

Presiding over all.

Nothing but carrion for statistics now, protective ribs now exposed,

Battered by dust and gnawing curiosity of those better than you by chance,

Kill A Man's Giro and doom him to nomadic, bewilderment of sanction,

And the famine of ill fame.

Internet Has Caught Me

The internet's been talking at me,
Murmuring slurry, bestowing vacuum,
Gravitationally locked into the e-portal,
Traversing alternate realms of IP and ID.

Lofty towers imprison recollections of grace,
Fibre optic panopticon scurry me away,
Lead me astray, floundering, inapt to adapt,
Remain cocooned on the tree of cyber-life.

Our connections rely on derivatives of glass,
Notions of existence shatter with greater aplomb,
When the vessel of all we knew, magnetism of true,
Breaks asunder with the lie of installed liberty.

Chatter deafens as I dial up the shrapnel of me,
A bookmark of worth lurks in the Multiverse,
Internet bestows with one click, thieves with another,
Crime lost in the ocean of trolling, miscellany, false mother.

Streaming notions hitchhike on the super highway,
To and fro, arcing lights in the cosmos of opinion and idea,
Trolls lurk under bridge ventured across with timid heart,
An essence stretched and frayed over cables and in profile.

Identity seeks sanctuary of the trough, uniqueness offered up,
As truffles unearthed by sows amid soil of conformity,
Regurgitated in the throes of oppressive sewage,
Virile stench of your own entrails illuminated on screen.

Broad bands of duct tape bind my wrists and essence,
Funnelled down the carpel tunnel, where is the light?
Blinded by the glare where we all become a sole type,
Under the thrall of the Times New Roman Empire.

We seek nothing at the font of all knowledge,
Declare war on the opinion of Joe Blogs,
The global village is far from short of idiots,
The memory of a fuller life lies one town over.

All of us betwixt filth and firmament are click bait,

Dangled on hooks for the sharks of consumerism,
Jaws close yet do you sense the bite to even wriggle?
Locate the lock to reverse your tether to the screen.

The matrix is a grid to connect for life until death,
But the shell produces sound when vacated,
Waves lash audibly against the walls once you,
And we all fall down and switch off the outside, true?

Nectar of Ideas

Nectar of ideas drip, genesis of action,
Pooling as blood on reactionary paper of doing,
Tangents divide, forks in the lightning of thinking.

With fervent passion I bud like cherry blossom,
Waltzing to the caprice of sun and breeze,
Yet I calcify, harden and crack beneath winter's savage discipline.

Rendered motionless alongside frost choked tundra,
Too petrified to wait for scents of blooms,
Splashes of rain, or a breath to claim as my own.

Inevitability of Fear

The inevitably of pain heralds and motions cause and effect,

Stuns heaven's naivety, engorges hell's gross nexus with desire,

We plan to be ourselves at the bookends of life's sickening roll call,

Though squander our grace on want's grasping knuckles.

There was once a myth called give and take,

Gods and monsters of our base foundation,

Each are offered to furies to counterbalance our slide,

Disappearing between here and there in the marsh of solipsism.

Stench of existence is entropy's whore,

Tested against greed, the oubliette of the soul,

Lost on Butterfly wings of individuality,

As we cry no more, denied a skeleton of our identity.

Immolate our dignity in lava pits of laissez faire,

Our effigies parody the vigour of choice,

While we vent our spleen on ghostly shores of bullshit,

And mutilate our minds in an abattoir of imitation.

What Difference Doth A Century Make?

1914...

"Dulce et Decorum est, pro Patria Mori?"

I am ill prepared for unyielding horror, but is this just me?

Heart is lodged in dread, coated in the western front's slag,

A day is a decade in this rancid bowel, home and trench,

Ticking down eras, from a time when normality and I were acquainted.

Glory was a spectral illusion to lure us here in droves,

King and country sit in peace, a commonwealth away,

Riches exceeding numerous filth coating uniform's muted green,

Woolly shade of nausea, banner of me and my German reflection's misdeeds.

Above the trench dwells man's best parallel of hell,

Melee of mud, barbed wire, wood corpses, meat I called mates,

Stench of mustard gas waltzes infernally over dying sorrow,

Grey sky, chill air litter the vista with my dulled aching fear.

Aligned on the verge is my company, akin and estranged comrades,

Death shares a canteen with us and dines on the unsaid between banter,

Lingering in those eager, weighs on those uncertain, drenches in rain as we go over,

Propelling duty, sinking teeth of boots into mud, adrenaline scarring reason.

Out of purgatory's trench these young tin soldiers elevate into perdition,

Hammering heart submerges external din, shielding raw horror from slaughter,

Mist and smoke invade and pervade, concealing barbed wire serpents,

Contriving to trap a free man, bind him in patriotic sacrifice,

Death is Almighty, smothering in declarations of erupting earth and dying screams.

Fear dulls senses, the concoction of an elixir of servitude in today's needles,

Potion of government issue martial action, military lambs to the slaughter,

Howling munitions & contrition flood me, as dirt flowers & domino soldiers fall,

Rifle my sole companion, memory of trench, unwelcome reminder of my distance.

Thudding pulse drives me forward, ringing smoke, dust and chaos drowns me,

Eyes stream, soul unconsciously weeps through horror, smoke and my reeking fear,

Agony & terror form discordant of human woe, deafened in this diabolical meadow,

Upon mustard gas, violent chorus turmoil has its throe, gunfire's banquet.

Froze amid anarchy's tapestry I study warfare's venomous grace,

Recalling an age ago, a quiet village, gentle sun, whiling freedom away,

Memories of love, spectres of me, thread the gossamer veils of desecration,

In my bubble, the battlefield of Flanders loses focus as I fight to remember peace,

Whip crack bite sinks into my rigid flesh, pain rears like the German ghosts afar,

Knees tremor, burning acid is my blood, veins like the
trenches scouring the fields,

Sinking into the mud, blood escapes with liberty, fog of war
lifts,

Face down, the mud greets the soldier, kindred spirits in
oppressed nations.

The letters I wrote home spring to mind as the ink of life ebbs
from me,

Messages of a planned and hoped for future now written as a
legacy in blood,

Cold seeps from mud and sky into veins as warfare gains
another legionnaire,

Earth is ashes, this 14-year-old glory hunter's lust is dust,
repatriated by death.

"Dulce et Decorum est, pro Patria Mori?"

You’re My Bucket List

You’re my bucket list,
You’re my key,
A division exists, persists,
But I am you, you are me.

You’re my bucket list,
You’re my key,
Turn my tide light,
When I’m savage, icy sea.

You’re my bucket list,
You’re my key,
Twist a blessed knife,
In the masochist gut of me.

You’re my bucket list,
You’re my key,
We both of us run,
But only I flee.

You're my bucket list,
You're my key,
Branch out in green hue,
Staining the shade of my tree.

You're my bucket list,
You're my key,
We are manacles,
That refuse the gift of free.

You're my bucket list,
You're my key,
A division exists, persists,
But I am you, you are me.

Estuary Movement

Thames Estuary, birth canal,

where ideas and influences charge,

a confluent rush to uterine docks in the capital,

once birthing Empire.

Adolescent of annex now spent,

The mind is more mature, yet,

The body-politic, callow, sputters aimless,

Devouring proletarian flame formed of tallow.

Body's intransigence yields to mind's acceptance,

An understanding of how the constant faunal gush of centuries,

A lunatic convergence of cultures and ideas on a global scale, plants a seed.

A seed in a locale the "leaders" would have us believe barren,

Instead we stand upon unencumbered, fecund meadows,

ripe with dormant growth, swelling ideas, art and creation.

Creativity is the hand slapping a drum beat on the soul,

We dance to the resonance, across the estuary hands lie amid those seeds.

They are grown from Grain to Gravesend,

Ceaseless bloom of vision,

Melded into the river's crucible,

Melded to the motion of the estuary.

About the Author

Brad James was born Bradley James Yellop in 1983 in London. Brad comes from a long line of creative individuals, including his great-uncle, Alec Gerard, who wrote for British sitcoms, and his great-aunt, Mary Brown, who has published two autobiographical novels. A prolific reader from a young age, Brad always possessed the ability - even whilst playing with friends and siblings as a child - to create his own Universe of characters and worlds, into which he would later adopt characters.

Brad took to writing at the age of ten, after reading *The Lord of the Rings* and beginning to write his own fan fiction. After an adolescent lull, Brad graduated from University. His love of the written word rekindled, he has been writing ever since. Having been highly moved and affected by the marked social injustice that has become glaring in the light of the recent recession, his musings converted to verse and poetry, as art is often the most subjective way to study the mood of the world.

Brad's active imagination has influenced him throughout his life, leading to the genesis of his novel, *The Fate of Orital: Volume One: The Return of the Mighty Ones*, which is nearing completion. He is also currently developing films.

38389988R00081

Made in the USA
Charleston, SC
05 February 2015